ELECTRICITY AND MAGNETS

Barbara Taylor

Photographs by Peter Millard

FRANKLIN WATTS

New York • London • Sydney • Toronto

Design: Janet Watson

Science consultant: Dr Bryson Gore

Primary science adviser: Lillian Wright

Series editor: Deborah Fox

Editor: Roslin Mair

The author and publisher would like to thank the following children for their participation in the photography of this book: Lauren Bennett, James Bennett, Daniel Kinsey, Thomas Kinsey, Asraf Mosaheb and Anushki Bodhinayake.
We are also grateful to Julia Edwards and Joy Mackey of Bounds Green Junior School, and Susan Kinsey. Thanks to Heron Educational Ltd for loaning equipment for use in the investigations.

Illustrations: Linda Costello

© 1990 Franklin Watts

Franklin Watts Inc.
387 Park Avenue South
New York
NY 10016

Library of Congress Cataloging-in-Publication Data

Taylor, Barbara, 1954-
Electricity and magnets / Barbara Taylor.
p. cm. — (Science starters)
Summary: Examines the similar properties of electricity and magnetism and demonstrates how electrical energy is generated to power household appliances.
ISBN 0-531-14083-0
1. Electricity — Juvenile literature. 2. Magnetism — Juvenile literature. [1. Electricity. 2 Magnetism.]
I. Title. II. Series.
QC527.2, T39 1990
537 — dc20   90–31021
                                  CIP AC

Printed in Belgium

CONTENTS

This book is all about how to make electricity, how electricity travels along wires, the forces around magnetic materials, and how we use electricity and magnets. It is divided into six sections. Each has a different colored triangle at the corner of the page. Use these triangles to help you find the different sections.

These red triangles at the corner of the tinted panels show you where a step-by-step investigation starts.

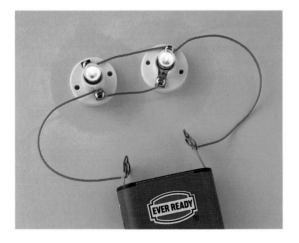
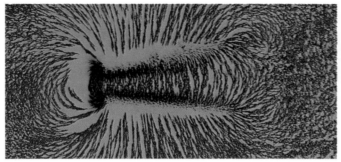

USING ELECTRICITY

Imagine what this city would look like if there was a power blackout.

Without electricity there would be no electric lights inside or outside the buildings. None of the electric equipment in people's homes and offices would be working. There would be no street lights or traffic lights to help drivers, and at night the city would be pitch black. People living in the city would find life very difficult.

Electricity is a form of energy, and can make things work. You can't see electricity, but you can see the effect it has on other things.

Have a look around your home or school. How many machines can you find that use electricity? The kitchen is a good place to start. Most of the electrical gadgets we rely on have been invented in the last 150 years. Before this, it used to take a very long time to cook, wash, and clean.

Before people discovered how to make electricity, they used the power of flowing water, the wind, or animals to make machines work. Their light and warmth came from the Sun, from fires, and from candles. Candles do not give out much light and the hot flame can easily start fires.

Have you ever played with a toy electric car? Inside the car is an electric motor, which contains magnets. The electricity and magnets work together to make the car move.

Many of the machines we use, such as hairdriers, have motors inside them to make them work. You can find out more about electric motors on page 26.

Some electrical things work without the help of magnets. A flashlight, for instance, uses the electricity made by a battery to light up the bulb. See how many battery-powered things you can find.

Magnets can also be very useful without electricity. The counters in the game shown here are magnetic and stick to the metal board. Even if the board is tipped up, the counters stay where they are and don't fall off. You can play games like this when you are traveling in a car, a bus, or a train where it may be hard to keep the board still.

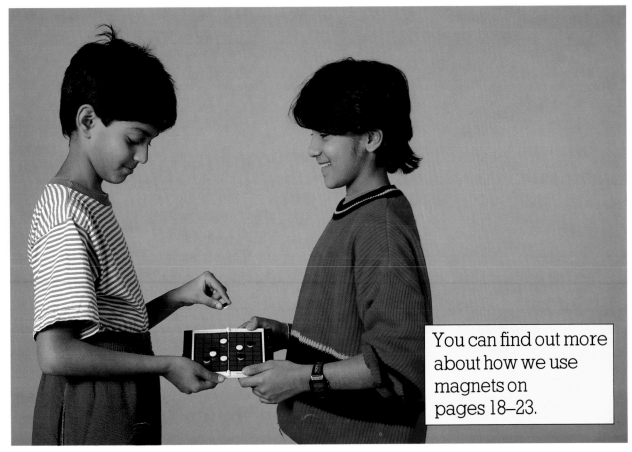

You can find out more about how we use magnets on pages 18–23.

SPARKS AND FLASHES

Rub a balloon hard against a wool sweater, then hold the balloon above your head. Can you make your hair stand on end? This happens because of static electricity, which is made by rubbing things together. It can pull things together or push them apart. The static electricity on the balloon pulls the hair toward it.

Try rubbing a comb on a wool sweater and then hold it next to a thin stream of water. The static electricity on the comb pulls the water and makes it bend toward the comb.

You can sometimes see little sparks of static electricity if you undress in the dark. The electricity is made by your clothes rubbing together. The spark is made by the electricity jumping up in the air.

Lightning is a huge spark of static electricity that has built up in storm clouds. It happens when little droplets of water and ice inside the cloud rub against each other. In a bad storm, the electricity jumps from one cloud to another, and sometimes jumps to the ground. Lightning is very powerful. It can damage trees or buildings and start fires. It can even kill people.

BATTERIES

Static electricity is not very useful for making machines work because it is hard to catch it and make it do things. The electricity we use every day can be controlled more easily. It can be made to move along inside wires and travel from place to place.

Electricity is carried by tiny particles called electrons. The marbles in this photograph represent the electrons inside a wire. The movement of electrons along a wire is called an electric current.

Electrical currents need a power source to make them flow. Power stations make the force that makes currents flow into homes and workplaces. Batteries can also cause currents to flow.

The electricity in a battery is made by chemical reactions. When the chemicals have been used up the battery is dead and has to be thrown away. But some batteries can be recharged to make the chemical reactions start up again. Electric wheelchairs run on rechargeable batteries.

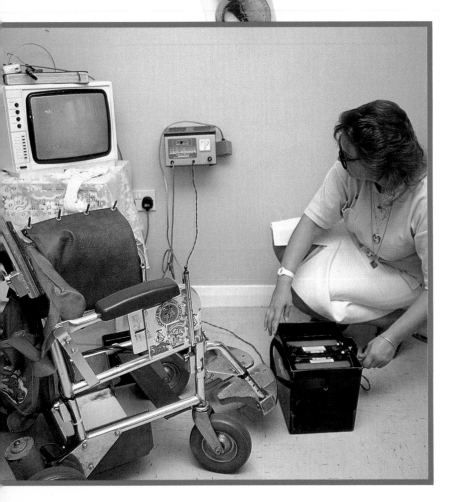

This cut-away view of a battery shows you what it looks like inside. The chemical reactions in a battery make negative charges (electrons) collect at one end and positive charges (protons) collect at the other end. This is why there are plus and minus signs on a battery.

Most batteries are safe to use for the investigations in this book. They are not usually as powerful as the electricity that comes out of a socket in the wall and they are small enough to be carried from place to place.

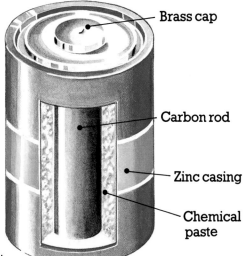

Brass cap

Carbon rod

Zinc casing

Chemical paste

Try making your own battery.

MOTIRIAL FOR A PENNY BATTERY

1 Cut up some blotting paper and aluminum foil into small pieces.

2 Soak the blotting paper in salty water.

3 Put a penny on the table with a piece of foil on top and a piece of salty blotting paper on top of that.

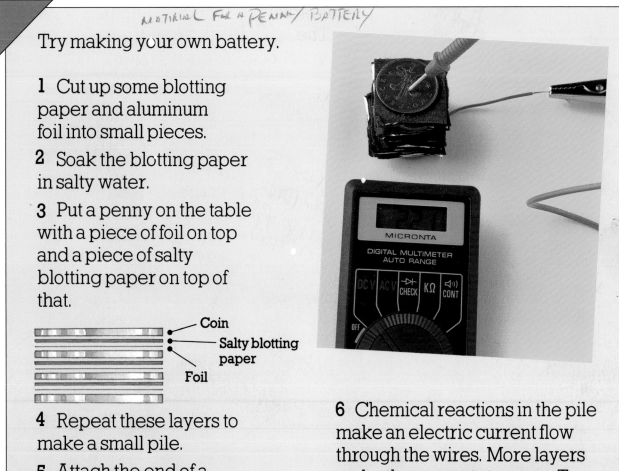

Coin

Salty blotting paper

Foil

4 Repeat these layers to make a small pile.

5 Attach the end of a piece of wire underneath the pile. Attach another wire on top.

6 Chemical reactions in the pile make an electric current flow through the wires. More layers make the current stronger. To measure the current, see if you can make a small bulb light up, as shown on the next page.

USE A VOLT METER

CIRCUITS

When electrons flow along a wire, the path they take is called a circuit. As long as there are no gaps in a circuit, the electrons keep moving along it. Can you make a simple circuit with a battery, two pieces of wire, and a small bulb?

The light comes on when the electricity from the battery goes out along the wire, through the bulb, and back along the other wire into the battery again.

To find out more about circuits, try wiring two bulbs into a circuit. There are two main ways of doing this.

One way is to put the bulbs in a row. This is called a series circuit. The bulbs are sharing the same electricity, so they give out a dim light. If you take one out, the other goes out too.

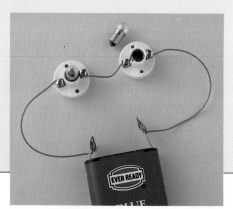

The electric lights on a Christmas tree are often wired in a series circuit. If one bulb goes, it makes a gap in the circuit. The electricity cannot reach the other bulbs, so all the lights go out.

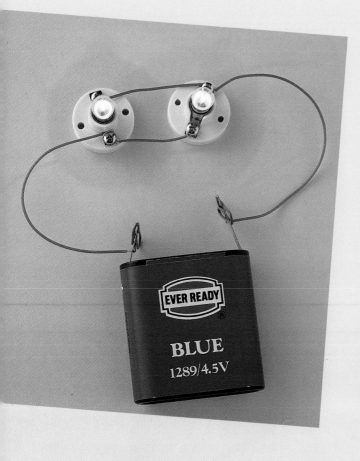

The other way is to give each bulb its own connection to the battery. If you remove a bulb now, it makes no difference to the other light.

CONDUCTORS AND INSULATORS

Which materials does electricity flow through? To find out, make a collection of things made of different materials

Then make a circuit with three wires, a battery, and a bulb. Leave a gap between two of the wires, and put each material in turn into the gap. When the circuit is complete, does the bulb light up?

Materials that let electricity flow through them are called conductors. Metals are good conductors. Materials that do not let electricity flow through them are called insulators. Make a list of the conductors and insulators in your collection.

Does water conduct electricity well? Why do bathrooms have to have special devices called Ground Fault Interrupter Circuits (GFICs)? This is because electricity and water together can be very dangerous. Water splashed onto wires that carry electricity could cause a severe electric shock.

We use conductors to carry electricity to where it is needed and insulators to prevent it from leaking, where it is not wanted. The insulators in this power station are made from porcelain. They look rather like piles of plates.

A plastic coating is used to insulate wires and keep the electricity from leaking out. Electricity flows along the copper wires inside the plastic.

If a wire needs to bend easily, it is made of many thin strands. These wires are called flexible cables. But if a wire will not need to move once it has been fitted, it has a thick strand of copper in the middle. These wires are called cables.

SWITCHES

When you press a light switch to turn it off, you make a gap in a circuit. The electricity stops flowing and the light goes out. When you press the switch on again, you complete the circuit. Electricity flows through to the bulb and makes it light up.

Try making a simple switch, like the one in the picture. Use a metal conductor, such as a paperclip, to switch the bulb on or off. It does not matter where you connect the switch into the circuit.

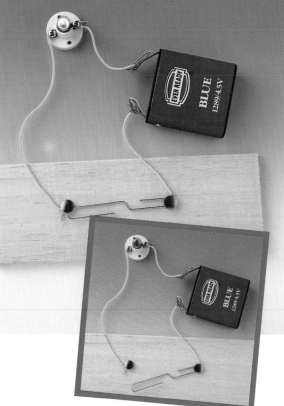

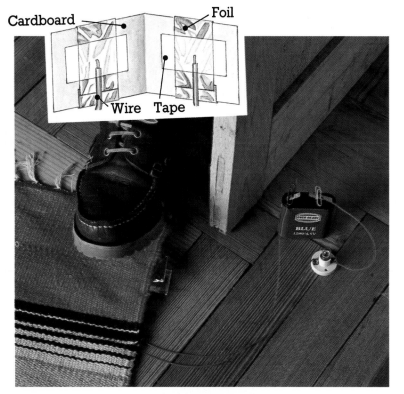

Cardboard — Foil

Wire   Tape

You can also make an alarm "switch". Fold a thin piece of cardboard in half and wrap a piece of aluminum foil around each end. Tape a wire to each piece of foil and join the wires to a battery and a bulb or a buzzer to make a circuit.

Hide the cardboard under a mat. When someone's foot presses the switch, this completes the circuit; the bulb lights, or the buzzer sounds.

RESISTANCE

The thin, glowing wire inside a light bulb is called the filament. The filament is very thin and the electricity has to push very hard to get through it. The pushing makes the filament so hot it glows brightly and gives out light. The wire is made of a metal that can get very hot without melting. It is coiled so that a lot of wire will fit into a small space inside the bulb and more light will be given out.

A thin wire reduces the flow of electricity. This effect is called resistance. It means that a thin wire can carry less electricity than a thick wire.

The length of a wire also affects its resistance. Like a wire, the graphite or "lead" in a pencil lets electricity flow through it. The shorter pencil has less resistance to the flow of electricity than the longer pencil. So it gives a lower reading on the resistance meter.

MAGNETIC FORCES

If you hold a magnet near a refrigerator door, you can feel it being pulled toward the door. When you let go, the magnet sticks to the door. Some materials have the power to pull other objects toward them. They are said to be magnetic. You cannot see how a magnet works, but you can have lots of fun playing with magnets.

Which sort of materials are magnetic objects made from? Make a collection of objects made from different materials, such as metal, glass, plastic, rubber, and wood. Test each object with your magnet and sort them into two groups – objects that are magnetic and objects that are not.

Keep magnets well away from watches, TVs, videos, and tape recorders. Magnets can damage these things and stop them working properly.

How strong are magnets? Some magnets are stronger than others. Test some different magnets and see how many paperclips each one will pick up. Are bigger magnets stronger than smaller magnets? Can you find the part of each magnet that has the most pulling power?

In the picture, can you see that some of the paperclips are sticking to the others? The magnetic field given out by the magnet has turned each paperclip into a little magnet. Each paperclip attracts some of the other clips.

The pull of a magnet is strongest at two points, called the magnetic poles. In a long, straight magnet (a bar magnet), the poles are at either end. If you tie a thread around a bar magnet, and hold the thread so that the magnet swings freely, it will come to rest with one end pointing to the Earth's North Pole and one end pointing to the Earth's South Pole. You can check this with a compass. The poles on a bar magnet are called North and South too. If you hold the North Pole and the South Pole of two magnets near each other, they will attract each other.

If you put two South Poles together, they will try to push each other apart or repel each other. A useful rule to remember is that the same poles repel each other and different poles attract each other. What happens if you put two North Poles together?

Magnets can be made in all shapes and sizes, from bars and horseshoes to circles. It is difficult to understand the pushing and pulling forces around magnets. But if you put a large sheet of paper on top of a magnet and sprinkle iron filings on the paper, you can see the pattern of the lines of force. More iron filings gather together where the magnet gives out a strong force. Where the force is weaker, the lines are further apart.

Round magnet

Horseshoe magnet

The pattern below was made by the horseshoe magnet on the right. Can you match up the other two patterns to the magnets in the picture above? The answer is on page 31.

1

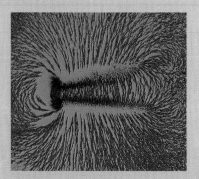

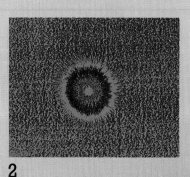

2

Magnetic window cleaners are very useful in places where it is hard to reach the outside of a window, such as tall buildings. One part of the cleaner goes outside the window and the other part goes inside. The two parts are held together by a strong magnet.

Magnetic window cleaners show that magnets can still work through glass. But other materials can block magnetic force. See if a magnet will attract a nail through a variety of materials.

Did you know that a compass needle is a magnet? People use compasses on maps to help them find their way. Compasses are used on ships and airplanes, as well as on land.

A compass needle always swings to point North because it is pulled by the magnetic force of the Earth (see page 30).

To find out how compasses work, make one yourself.

1 First you need to make a needle magnetic. To do this, stroke a needle with one end of a magnet. Make sure you stroke it in the same direction each time and hold the magnet away after each stroke. The more times you stroke the needle, the more powerful your magnetic needle will be. Be careful with your magnet. If you drop it or bang it hard, it will lose its magnetic power.

2 Put some water in a saucer.

3 Ask an adult to help you cut a thin slice from a piece of cork.

4 Put your magnetic needle on top of the cork and float the cork in the saucer.

5 Use the Sun, a local map or a real compass to check that your compass needle is pointing North.

ELECTRO-MAGNETS

When a wire carrying electricity comes near a compass needle, a surprising thing happens. The compass needle moves. This happens because the electricity moving in the wire makes the wire magnetic.

Try this test to see how electricity can turn a nail into a magnet. This is called an electromagnet.

1 Wrap some plastic-coated wire tightly around a long nail. Leave both ends of the wire free.

2 Join the wires to a battery.

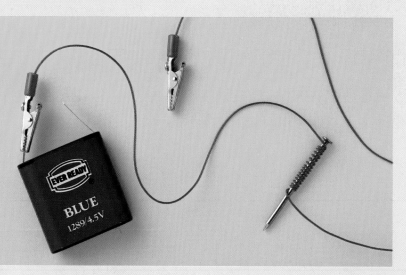

3 When electricity flows through the nail, it becomes a magnet. See how many paperclips your electromagnet will pick up.

4 If you wind more wire around the nail, does this make it into a stronger electromagnet?

5 If you take the wires off the battery, you break the circuit and stop electricity reaching the nail. So it stops being magnetic.

Electromagnets are very useful because they are only magnetic when the electricity is switched on. They can be turned off when they are not being used. They can also be very strong magnets. They are used in industry in many different ways.

Powerful electromagnets are used to pick out magnetic metals from piles of mixed trash. The magnet is attached to a crane, which lifts the magnet and the metal that is stuck to it. When the magnet is in position above the spot where the metal is being collected, the electricity is switched off and the metal falls off the magnet.

GENERATORS AND MOTORS

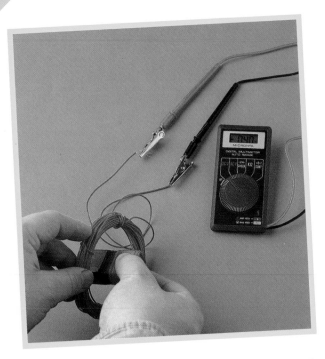

If electricity can make magnets, can magnets make electricity? If a coil of wire is connected to a meter that detects electric current, and then a magnet is pushed in and out of the coil, it should be possible to detect an electric current in the wire. When the magnet is still, no current is produced. Some generators use magnets and movement to make electricity.

An electric motor works in the opposite way. It uses magnetism and electricity to create movement. The electric motor in the picture is being used to move a model propeller.

Inside an electric motor are coils of wire on a rod or axle with a magnet around them. When an electric current is passed through the coils, it makes them magnetic. The magnets and coils push and pull each other and make the axle turn around. The important point to remember about motors is that they make things move.

Most of the electricity we use is made by huge generators in power stations like the one in the picture. The electric current from a power station is carried along a network of thick cables to reach our homes, schools, offices, and factories. Some of the cables are buried under the ground and some are held above the ground on tall towers called pylons. The electricity in these cables is very dangerous; it is more economical to move electric power at a very high pressure or voltage.

Never go near electricity pylons, overhead cables or electricity substations. The powerful electricity can easily jump across a gap and kill you.

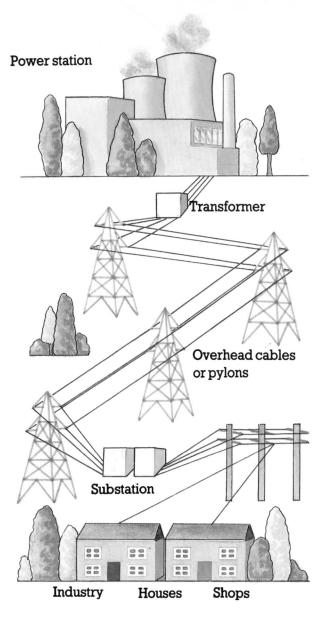

Power station

Transformer

Overhead cables or pylons

Substation

Industry   Houses   Shops

Before you can use the electricity in your home, to power a cassette player for instance, it has to be reduced to a lower, safer voltage. This job is carried out by devices called transformers in electricity substations.

Electricity is such an important part of our lives it is hard to imagine living without it. But it is also very dangerous. Always take care to use it safely.

27

MORE THINGS TO DO

Electronic quiz game

You can use your knowledge of circuits to make a quiz game. Make up some questions and answers and write each answer and each question on a separate piece of paper. Stick the questions and answers on one side of a large piece of cardboard, putting the wrong answer beside each question.

Push a paper fastener through the cardboard next to each question and each answer. On the back, attach a short piece of wire to each paper fastener. Attach the other end of each piece of wire to the fastener behind the right answer. With some more wire, make a circuit with a battery and a bulb. Leave two ends of wire free.

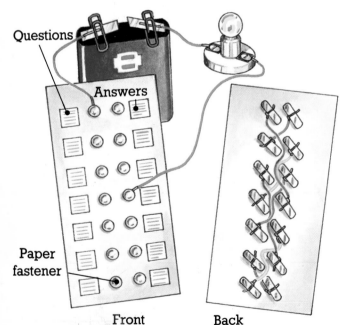

Front   Back

Ask a friend to use the wires to join up a question with the answer he or she thinks is the right one. If the answer is correct, they will complete a circuit, and the bulb will light up.

Magnetic boats

Make some little boats from pieces of cork. Press a thumbtack into the bottom of each boat. For the mast and sails, push a steel pin through a triangular piece of paper and stick the pin into the cork.

Tape or tie a small magnet to one end of some thread or string. Tie the other end of the thread or string to a stick or garden stake. Float the boats in a large bowl of water or in the bath and use the magnetic rods to pull the boats along. You could have magnetic boat races with your friends.

Electricity and heat

Electricity can make things work to give us heat. For instance, kettles and electric heaters give out heat. How many other electrical devices can you think of that give out heat? Some of them are used on farms, in factories, and in greenhouses.

Make an electric motor

Make a model of an electric motor to look like the one in the picture.

The electricity makes the wire magnetic. The wire reacts with the magnets and makes the polystyrene turn around.

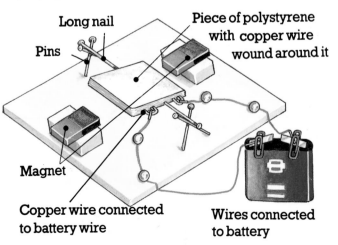

Two-way switch

At home or at school, do you have a light that can be switched off from either upstairs or downstairs? This needs a special switch called a two-way switch. It is useful because it allows a light to be turned on or off from different places. Make one of the switches yourself to see how it works.

You will need two switches, like the ones in the picture. See if you can draw diagrams to record the circuit for each switch when it is on or off.

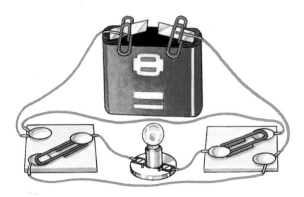

Battery power

What happens if you link more than one battery into a circuit with a light bulb? Do the extra batteries make the bulb glow more brightly?

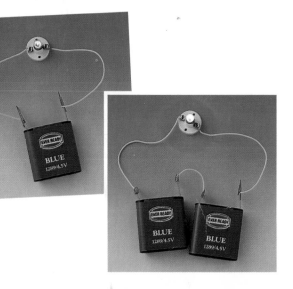

Make a lighthouse

Pull the top off a clean, dry, empty dishwashing liquid bottle, and cut off the bottom of the bottle. Cut two pieces of wire that are both about six inches longer than the bottle, and join one wire to either side of a small bulb holder. Screw a bulb into the holder, then push the holder up inside the bottle so the bulb comes out of the top. Tape or glue the holder in place.

Join one wire to a switch and the other wire to one end of a battery. Use a new piece of wire to join the switch to the other end of the battery. Fix your lighthouse upright in some modeling clay. Stick a clear glass or plastic cover over the bulb.

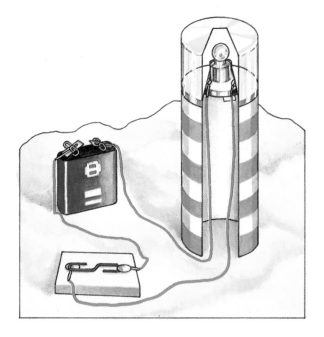

You can decorate your lighthouse if you like and put some stones around the bottom. Press the switch on and off to make the light flash. The flashing light on a real lighthouse warns ships of dangerous rocks and seas. Lighthouses save lives.

DID YOU KNOW?

▲ Static electricity was first discovered by the Greeks in about 600 BC. They made jewelery from a material called amber, which is the sap from trees that has become hard. The Greeks found that if you rubbed the amber with some cloth, the cloth attracted small objects. The Greek word for amber is elektron, so the force they discovered was called electricity.

▲ Some electric light is produced without making a wire filament glow. In fluorescent strip lights, an electric current is passed along a tube of gas. This makes the gas glow and give out light. Different gases produce different colored light. Neon makes red light, sodium makes yellow light, and mercury makes blue light.

▲ Magnets were discovered by the Greeks more than 2000 years ago. They found a type of black stone that attracted iron nails and pins. The stone was named magnetite, after Magnesia, the place where the stone was found. Magnesia was a part of modern-day Turkey.

▲ The magnetic North Pole is about 1000 miles away from the true North Pole. And the magnetic South Pole is about 1500 miles away from the true South Pole. People using compasses have to remember this when they figure out the direction of true North. Scientists have found that the Earth's magnetic poles move a few inches each year. In the past, magnetic North has sometimes even pointed South. The strength of the Earth's magnetic field is also constantly changing.

▲ The number of electrons in a piece of wire 0.4 × 0.4 × 4 inches is 100,000,000,000,000,000,000,000. This is more stars than there are in our galaxy, more than all the humans that have every lived, and more than all the animals in the world.

▲ The amount of electrical energy used by a 100 watt light bulb in ten hours would be enough to boil seven quarts of water, drill holes for four hours, run a color television for three hours, or clean carpets for two hours.

▲ The electric current from a power station is constantly changing direction. It goes backward and forward about 50-60 times every second. It is called alternating current (a.c.). A.c. is used for power lines because it can be sent more cheaply, is safer and is more efficient for most purposes than direct current (d.c.), such as the current from a battery.

▲ A light bulb glows as hot as 5000°F. It is filled with a gas that helps to stop the filament from burning away too quickly. The filaments in the first light bulbs were made from cotton or bamboo.

▲ The nervous system in our bodies depends on tiny electric currents to pass messages from sense organs, such as our eyes, to the brain and back to our muscles. These currents travel at speeds of up to 328 feet per second.

▲ An electric eel can produce massive electric shocks of 500 volts, which are powerful enough to kill a horse.

GLOSSARY

Alternating current (a.c.)
An electric current that flows first in one direction, then in another. Electricity from power lines is alternating current.

Battery
A package of chemicals that produces and stores electricity.

Circuit
A pathway for electricity to flow around. An electric current will not flow unless a circuit is complete.

Conductor
A material that allows electricity to flow through it easily. Copper and aluminum are both good conductors.

Direct current (d.c.)
An electric current that flows in one direction only. A battery produces d.c.

Electric current
The movement of electrons along a wire.

Electric motor
A machine that converts electricity into movement.

Electromagnet
An iron rod with many coils of wire wrapped around it. When an electric current is passed through the wire, the rod becomes a magnet.

Electron
One of the tiny particles of which matter is made. It has a negative charge. Moving electrons are what we call electricity.

Generator
A machine that produces electricity from movement. Generators in power stations produce only a.c.

Insulator
A material that does not let electricity flow through it easily. Plastic is a good insulator.

Magnetic poles
The places on a magnet where the magnetic pull is strongest.

Resistance
The opposition to the flow of an electric current. The more resistance a wire has, the less current it can carry.

Static electricity
A form of electricity produced when some materials are rubbed together.

Transformer
A device used to increase or decrease electrical voltage.

Voltage
The force that pushes electricity through a wire. The higher the voltage, the bigger the electric current.

Answer for p.21:
1 bar magnet
2 round magnet

INDEX

Additional photographs:
Chris Fairclough 4, 10 (b);
Hutchison Library 13 (t); Rex
Features 25 (br); Science Photo
Library 15 (t); ZEFA 9.
Picture researcher:
Sarah Ridley